House Beautiful

Decorating Solutions *for* SMALL SPACES

The Editors of House Beautiful Magazine

Text by Christine Pittel

HEARST BOOKS

A Division of Sterling Publishing Co., Inc.

NEW YORK

Copyright © 1998 by Hearst Communications, Inc.

This book was previously published as a hardcover under
the title *House Beautiful Small Spaces*.

Produced by Smallwood & Stewart, Inc., New York City
Editor: Laurie Orseck
Designer: Susi Oberhelman

Library of Congress Cataloging-in-Publication Data
Available upon request.

10 9 8 7 6 5 4 3 2 1

First Paperback Edition 2003
Published by Hearst Books
A Division of Sterling Publishing Co., Inc.
387 Park Avenue South, New York, NY 10016

House Beautiful and Hearst Books are trademarks
owned by Hearst Magazines Property, Inc., in USA, and
Hearst Communications, Inc., in Canada.

www.housebeautiful.com

Distributed in Canada by Sterling Publishing
c/o Canadian Manda Group, One Atlantic Avenue, Suite 105
Toronto, Ontario, Canada M6K 3E7

Distributed in Australia by Capricorn Link (Australia) Pty. Ltd.
P.O. Box 704, Windsor, NSW 2756 Australia

Manufactured in China

ISBN 1-58816-300-8

CONTENTS

foreword   9

introduction   11

ILLUSION OR REALITY   13

SCALE AND BALANCE   39
the editing process

COLOR AND PATTERN   59
white and beyond

SLEIGHT OF HAND   79
mirrors, air, and light

INVENTING SPACE   99
finding room, making room

DOUBLE DUTY   119
one-room living, dual-purpose spaces

GREAT SPACES   135
five ingenious solutions

design directory   172

photography credits   173

index   175

acknowledgments   176

foreword

This book is about a simple problem: having less space than you might like. But over the years, those of us who create the design stories in *House Beautiful* magazine month after month have learned a simple truth—although space has always been considered one of life's luxuries, less of it often produces the more ingenious design solutions.

As the pages to follow will illustrate, in the hands of a knowledgeable design practitioner space can expand or contract, and there are myriad ways to make the most of whatever you may have. You can play with paint, or paintings, to give a small room the excitement larger ones often take for granted; a major piece of furniture can work in the tiniest of rooms; and with little floor space you can always reach up to make the most of modest proportions. We all have learned that paring down, using only one color—especially shades of white—and organizing and editing what we have does help. But, on the other hand, saturated color, piles of things, and a quirky sense of style can prove so winsome that no one gives a thought to size.

'On the other hand' is the operative phrase when tackling small spaces. Valid solutions that seem at first to be contradictory simply reveal that decorating is first of all an art, not a science, and that rules are often made to be broken.

No one seems to grasp this better than the writer of *Decorating Solutions for Small Spaces,* Christine Pittel, who brings an amazing amount of experience and knowledge about design and decoration to this project—and perhaps, more importantly, wit and style as well. It takes all of that, as you will see, to make small spaces work, delight, and enhance the lives of those who live within them.

The Editors
House Beautiful

introduction

Let there be space. Open, generous, high-ceilinged space is the exception rather than the rule these days. Such material comforts as fine silk or polished mahogany are not half so rare as ample, beautifully proportioned rooms. But those of us confined to more compact quarters should keep in mind one heartening fact. As every designer worth his tape measure knows, the size of a room is as much a matter of perception as square footage.

In the eye of the beholder, space can expand or contract. In this elasticity lies the possibility of invention. Some space-swelling strategies are borrowed from design history, others are born out of sheer wit and desperation at the drafting table, and many are poured straight from a paint can.

The first decision for anyone facing a small room is fundamental: Do you want to make a tight space appear larger, or should you acquiesce to the snug dimensions and cultivate coziness? If creating an illusion of roominess is the answer, then sleights of pattern or color can work magic. So can editing—tame the anarchy of possessions. Brandish mirrors. Widen a room with strong horizontal lines, heighten it with verticals, stretch it with diagonals. Or choose the opposite approach—give in to reality and divide and conquer, packing everything you own into a crowded jumble that proves the counterintuitive Chinese principle that space expands when subdivided. Search for infinity in the infinitesimal.

The most audacious designers might just forget the measurements altogether and change the subject, whisking the eye into a fantasy world with shocks of color or an operatic piece of furniture. The bigger the lie, the larger the space.

Don't be cowed by meager dimensions. Be clever. No beautiful windows in your apartment? Try cove lighting instead. Light is the medium of mystery and revelation in space, and controlling it conjures magic and sets the tone of a room. As Italian painters who mastered chiaroscuro have long known, shadow is light's handmaiden. No wonder so many people like to panel a study and isolate themselves in a pool of lamplight, where a spirit of contemplation reigns and space dissolves in thought.

Architecture history books are full of classic solutions to spatial squeeze. Mies van der Rohe's Farnsworth House outside of Chicago, a rectangle of glass that hovers above the flood plain, is bounded primarily by reflections. No one pays much attention to square footage when the rooms inside this small masterpiece merge into trees and sky. Then there is that great prestidigitator of space, Frank Lloyd Wright, who made ordinary-size rooms grand by creating narrow, low-ceilinged antechambers to pass through before the release into more generous spaces that flow out of sight. Space is relative: Small is smaller, and big becomes bigger when each is juxtaposed to the other.

But you don't need an architectural degree to make the most of your measurements. The strategies illustrated on the following pages offer a head start on how to take space into your own hands.

illusion or REALITY

When it comes to small spaces, illusion is design's heavy lifter. There is power in duplicity done well. When designers white out the walls, floor, and ceiling, they obliterate the boundaries of a cramped room. Once the container disappears, furniture holds forth and exerts greater impact. Short, slim chairs can balloon the size of a space or, conversely, a monumental armchair can trick the eye into thinking the room, too, is on the same scale. The subterfuge of using the same color or pattern throughout—like camouflage—will make objects merge into the larger whole. And meandering layouts expand the impression of space.

Some people prefer to tell the truth. No matter what the size of their space, they capitulate to reality and simply steep themselves in the comfort of things they love. They may take advantage of every available surface, arranging countless tablescapes and covering the walls with prints ceiling high. If you've got it, flaunt it.

Then there are those free radicals who defy their confines by saturating the walls with hallucinogenic color to turn a small room into a three-dimensional Matisse. After all, reality is only a state of mind.

Japanese gardeners are famous for borrowing space from the larger landscape. The same concept applies to interiors, which can expand through a borrowed view. At first glance, a wall in this living room designed by Stephen Shubel (opposite) becomes a doorway, with a woman reading in the light of the window beyond. But the scene is in fact a painting—unlike this four-year-old's bedroom (above). Since it lacked a window, architect Walter Chatham cut a hole through to the kitchen and installed a salvaged sash so his daughter could have her own view. Shipshape bunk beds and floor-to-ceiling shelves pack a lot of toys and books into one cabin-size room.

Instead of fighting the diminutive dimensions of this Long Island farmhouse, the owners decided to yield to them, relaxing the rooms with easy chairs and just enough clutter to be cozy. Space-swelling strategies like the checkered floor painted on a diagonal (above) were more intuitive than calculated. To accommodate their furniture, they removed a wall dividing this room in two. One toile-covered armchair rambles over to the low-maintenance, galvanized tin-topped table (opposite) and links the dining and living areas. Two ample sofas (overleaf), rather than a crowd of chairs, face each other in front of the fireplace. Paintings are casually propped against every available surface; leaves from a Victorian pressed-fern album fill one wall.

Photographer David Livingston was stuck with a boring 1960s box for a bedroom—low ceiling, small window—so he decided to change the subject and coax the eye away from its flaws. Now there's a virtual canopy over his iron bed (opposite). "It's something you can do with a quart of paint and forty minutes," says the ad hoc decorator, who playfully draped his ties over a bamboo ladder rather than relegating them to the closet. Above: A room without views was no problem for New York designer Sheila Camera Kotur, who expanded the horizons of this small East Hampton carriage house by flanking an existing window with a trompe-l'oeil pair. Muralist Sara Nesbitt's imaginary panorama of palm trees and sailboats was inspired by the paintings Matisse did from his window overlooking the bay in Nice.

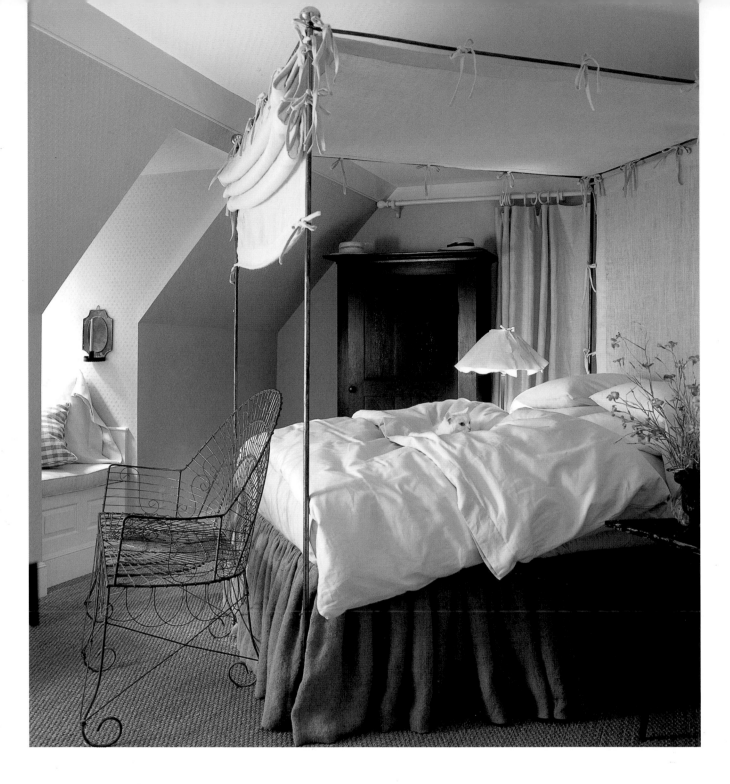

Atlanta designer Nancy Braithwaite has always seen the Shaker-like beauty of plain and simple things, so it's no surprise that coarse burlap becomes a down-to-earth dust ruffle on her daughter's bed (above). "All the character had to come from the bed, since this tiny upstairs bedroom had none of its own," says the designer. She made a queen-size iron bed the focal point of the room by placing it at an angle. Then she upped the impact with a linen canopy—tied on, for flexibility—and added a whimsical iron chair, for fun. Opposite: Who cares if a room is small and dreary when you can wake up in an exotic bed? At night, in the glow of the lantern with the striped curtains closed, it becomes a room within a room—a magic carpet ride into the Casbah.

A definite dearth of wall space in his Maine cabin didn't stop Boston designer Gregory D. Cann. He just went vertical, running a series of botanical prints over the living room/dining room window and topping it with a pyramid of plates under the gable (opposite). Hang 'em high could also be decorator Sam Blount's motto. In his 1825 farmhouse in upstate New York (above), he hung framed silhouettes clothesline-style at the top of the living room walls. Hand-hewn beams bring down the ceiling, a strategy that draws the eye up the full nine-foot height of the room. It also turns the collection into an architectural element, giving the room the visual continuity of a crown molding (overleaf).

fancy free

Sheep once slept here, which is part of the problem with acquiring a 400-year-old farmhouse—the rooms are tiny and the windows even tinier. Back then, people in the South of France built thick stone walls against the drowsy summer heat and fierce winds of winter and husbanded whatever warmth they could stoke from their fireplaces. The defensive mentality built into the closed cavelike forms of these picturesque abodes differs from the optimistic openness of houses today.

Enter couturier Michel Klein and his associate, Joel Fournier, two smart Parisians with attitude. Not for them the cheerful little floral prints associated with the sunny Midi; nor would they bother with the major structural changes an architect might favor. These break-out home-owners started with a different premise: the house as a canvas and color as salvation.

The two set the stakes high by starting with hues that would humble Matisse. Burnt orange, saffron, turquoise, Aegean blue—sponged, dappled, ragged, or lapped on with a brush—would be the background. These color addicts

The stygian ground floor of this 1595 Provençal farmhouse, where the animals once roamed, has acquired a sunburst of color—but not through the stunted windows. Michel Klein and Joel Fournier painted the vaults top to bottom in a sunflower yellow so intense that the furniture basks in its glow. Then they added to the ambient light by serving up mismatched patterns on the breakfast table (opposite) under a wrought-iron chandelier studded with flame-red candles. A door near the dining table (above), decorated with a fantasy overdoor imported from some nonexistent exotic country, conveys the cartoonish charm of a stage set.

found their pigments on a bicycle ride to the local shop and mixed the powders in standard acrylic paint diluted to washy transparency with water.

Once liberated, twice free: Fauvist painting became Fauvist decorating. The two homeowners binged at antiques stores and flea markets, carting back everything from the worthless to the valuable and mixing it all up with eclectic fervor: Louis XV, meet a barbarically bold kilim. What they didn't own and couldn't buy they simply painted—pigments of their imagination. Overdoors were acquired for the price of a coat of chrome yellow; crown moldings were sketched in grease pencil. In short, the somber interiors got a life through the pure power of fantasy and its handmaiden, paint. Klein and Fournier created a saucy interior world that completely opens up the old house. The sun comes in via bursts of color.

Fournier's blue-sponged bedroom (opposite) is a portrait of insouciance. A squiggly line weaving through dots passes for a crown molding and accentuates the height of the room, reflected in a stately Venetian mirror resting on a mantelpiece tiled with a riot of broken china. A painted chest lives by its wit in a room otherwise furnished with variations on Louis XVI. Above: The fearless homeowners mixed design messages in the dining area with a serious table draped in a sporty checkerboard cloth and surrounded picnic-style by standard French garden chairs. Beams painted chrome yellow draw the eye up.

Klein and Fournier spread red on the walls of a guest bedroom (above). An embroidered Indian shawl acting as an informal bedspread holds its own under a canopy of dramatically draped Balinese batiks. Sketches of St. Tropez flank a Venetian mirror hanging over a curvaceous nineteenth-century settee. Fragments of a matador's costume are framed on the adjoining wall. Opposite: A klatch of furniture busily keeps its own mixed company in an alcove ripe for reverie. The nonchalant grouping is as picturesquely composed as the painting over the window.

calm and collected

The 1846 shingled house on Long Island was as unprepossessing as they come when Tricia Foley bought it. But the style-book author synonymous with colorless color schemes was undaunted. After all, this is the woman who can make a cardboard egg carton look poetic.

Foley started the renovation of her country cottage by ripping out the fake knotty-pine paneling and faux-grain linoleum floors reminiscent of "a 1960s basement rec room" and replastering and repainting until she had a clean shell. In a 900-square-foot house that gives new meaning to the word *cozy* (one twin bed took up half the bedroom), her strategy was simple—white it out. "If you repeat the same colors from room to room a small house feels seamless," she explains. "The eye blurs the boundaries instead of stopping at each new color, so you create the illusion of more space." Even in an all-white room, there are a hundred different shades of pale. "I see china white, linen white, Navaho white, oyster white," she says, surveying the living room.

Beautiful objects keep finding their way into Foley's orbit, and she has no intention of living without them. The reality of keeping her possessions all around her means a certain amount of well-composed clutter. But something interesting happens when there's a consistency to the collections: Suddenly, you appreciate all the various shades and textures—from creamware's milky glaze to the flaking paint on a farmhouse table—subsumed in that one word, white.

When people sigh about how white and perfect her Long Island country house looks, Tricia Foley knows better. "Actually, it's off-white and imperfect," she laughs. Benjamin Moore #1535, a warm gray paint, softens the living room (opposite) where old French shutters along the wall are often pulled into the kitchen just beyond to screen off the cooking mess from the nearby dining table. Foley installed the wide plank floors and the Georgian-style paneling—made with plywood and stock molding—around the fireplace (above). The rough trestle table (overleaf), which now collects coffee cups and books, once held a washtub. Since it's merely an outline in space it doesn't bulk up the room.

A wall-to-wall mahogany sleigh bed, circa 1810, just squeezed into the bedroom (above). Swathed in mosquito netting hung from cup hooks in the ceiling— "I was going through my British Colonial phase," says Foley—it becomes an ethereal vision. An exquisitely embroidered tablecloth moonlights as a coverlet. In the bathroom (opposite), vintage hand towels hang on peg racks. The old-fashioned sink is draped in khaki trouser fabric. No plastic shower curtain hooks will do here: Muslin is tied onto a wooden dowel and falls delicately down beside the Shaker chair.

scale and BALANCE

The Aborigines have a saying, "The more you know, the less you need." For the wise and experienced eye, decorating is often a matter of paring down to a few good things. Sometimes people need a nudge from a professional in order to be sufficiently ruthless. "If the three key words in real estate are 'Location, location, location,' the three key words in design are 'Edit, edit, edit,'" observes designer Celeste Cooper. "If in doubt, leave it out."

The result in a small room can be striking: Suddenly space inflates. Relieved of the pressure of congestion, each piece has room to breathe. That special antique chair or cherished table acquires statuesque presence when its fine lines are silhouetted against clear, clean backdrops. Lilting curves thrive when surfaces are quieted with solid colors rather than competitive patterns.

In a room reduced to essentials, each object left standing must be able to bear the scrutiny. For less than perfect furniture, clutter offers convenient camouflage. There is an art to proliferation, and decorating for profusion instead of spareness constitutes another form of editing. Filling a room with objects can be very provocative, especially if the objects are all variations on a theme. A collection of botanical prints can look spectacular—hung multiply, framed simply or not at all. Quantity can be as captivating as quality.

Distill style down to its essence and it might look like this: strong lines, intriguing shapes, and a hint of color. Decorating editor Dara Caponigro bolted a neoclassical mantel to the wall and made a nondescript Manhattan foyer memorable (opposite). Simple white plates line up like sculpture, and chairs chosen for character carry on their own conversation. Above: Designer Sue McGregor composed a contemporary table and two nineteenth-century French pine children's chairs into a serene still life in her Washington, D. C. dining room. Overleaf: The cool pearl-gray color scheme chosen by designers Charles Spada and Tom Vanderbeck for a Connecticut living room sets off white window trim, which accentuates the room's height. Framed intaglios hang on brass gallery rods, and the coffee table is a see-through acrylic curve.

Inevitably, many of the drawings and engravings Roger Lussier shows in his framing shop and gallery migrate to his own genteel apartment in Boston's Back Bay. Hung nineteenth-century-style on the wall (opposite), suspended from ribbons or propped on the mantel (above), the overflowing collection is subtly unified by the gleam of gilt frames that reflect the light. Walls and furniture are neutralized with paint and upholstery in evanescent shades of gray and white so that the pictures become the environment. Even a small drawing gains stature when framed like a jewel, floating in a vast expanse of cream matting.

There's fascination, as well as safety, in numbers. In their weekend house on the fringe of the Ozark Mountains in Arkansas, one family brought the outside in by papering the living room with Redouté and Audubon prints they found in a used bookstore. The single motif, multiplied, gives the room its personality. Flowers drop off the walls onto the upholstery (opposite). Some of the birds can be seen in the woods framed by the picture window (above). The thematic design melts the room into a reverie about the nature these city dwellers sought in the hills. "I worried it would close up the house, but in fact it opens it by giving a sense of the world beyond," says the owner. "What saves it from monotony is that all the prints are different."

block party

Architects, notoriously, cannot afford their own work, or at least not much of it, so when they do design for themselves, the buildings tend to be small. In sprawling, big-house Houston, Carlos Jimenez makes the most of his own two-bedroom structure by emphasizing volume. The 20 by 40-foot shoebox has a modest footprint, but the flat roof allowed him to add the height that would have been lost under more traditional sloping gables to the living spaces on the second floor. The kitchen, sitting area, and dining area at the top of a slim flight of stairs feel generous. "By reversing the normal order and placing the two bedrooms on the ground floor, I expanded the scope of the living area," says the architect. "I now can look out over the trees."

Jimenez is not so much a minimalist as an architect of simplicity, taking care to strip interiors of anything extraneous, such as baseboards, moldings, and unnecessary trim. Without any distinguishing details or surface decoration, the blank walls seem to recede into the distance, leaving only a wide expanse of floor. And he likes his space cubed: Bedrooms become magnificently empty voids contained within a basic cube, like the blocks of space you would expect to find inside a rudimentary *Monopoly* house. "I've

With elemental directness and austerity, Carlos Jimenez arranges a tablescape of objects (opposite) in the same way he deploys furniture in a room—against neutral backgrounds, surrounded with plenty of breathing space to reveal form and bring out character. The stucco facade of his house (above) is so simple that the ephemera of the day—the shadows of leaves, the movement of branches—registers on its plain white surface like a visual haiku. Windows punched into it indicate the placement of rooms inside: The big three-over-three window gives the living area a glimpse of the city skyline, and the discrete square on the left marks the dining area.

always felt that simplicity is the most complex of human endeavors, and the hardest to achieve," says Jimenez.

Within this pure void, the architect floats furniture in zones that define how the empty space will be used. Seating arrangements rather than walls organize the space. And no ordinary furniture will do, of course; Jimenez instead chooses talismans carefully culled from twentieth-century architectural history—an Eames sofa, Mies van der Rohe ottomans, Thonet chairs. The pieces are all leggy—they lift their bodies off the floor so that space passes through uninterrupted. No carpet anchors each group, which Jimenez holds together only by notions of right-angled geometry. He clusters furniture toward the center of the room to surround it with space. Sculptural contours read beautifully in the quiet clarity. The furniture in turn suits the space: the low lines cede height to the room itself.

Jimenez, who hails from Costa Rica, uses color sparingly but boldly—usually just a field of color on the walls of one room set within another room. "I often think of architecture as a still life of shapes in space," he explains. In his deliberate approach to color, he follows in the footsteps of renowned Mexican architects Luis Barragan and Ricardo Legorretta, and all the anonymous builders in Latin America who paint the doors of their whitewashed houses shocking pink or cerulean blue. Within his geometrically plain, highly disciplined interiors, a turquoise wall defining the kitchen proves that Jimenez knows when to let go.

An arrangement of bookshelves rather than a wall **separates the living area from the staircase.** Within a neutral white shell that contains a neatly defined volume of space, Jimenez arranges contemporary classics such as Oscar Tusquets and Arne Jacobsen chairs. The stripped-down walls approach the neutral simplicity of an art gallery, with the similar

effect of isolating and emphasizing each object on its own visual terms. The wall around the kitchen is painted turquoise (overleaf) so that it "becomes another piece of furniture," says the architect. In this controlled context, the views framed by perfectly positioned windows resemble fragments of a landscape painting.

With unruly appliances and protruding cabinets, the kitchen characteristically is the most difficult room in a house to master visually. But by choosing white cabinets and recessing the refrigerator, Jimenez stills the space (opposite). The half-height wall allows for interaction, while a granite modesty panel "keeps a certain level of privacy for the pots." A polished concrete floor gives added depth to the cloud-white bedroom (above), brought down to earth by a Le Corbusier chaise and a television. The light is filtered by the architect's favorite mini-blinds. "They add another silhouette, and permit fantastic variations from sharp to soft light," he says.

hide in plain sight

Unable to repress his acquisitive instincts, designer Greg Jordan disciplined his tiny Manhattan apartment instead. Faced with a tight 13 by 16-foot living room and 10 by 15-foot bedroom, he decided to apply a variation of the camouflage principle: cover everything with the same pattern and it will seem to disappear. "I tried to come up with an American, urban version of those eighteenth-century English trellis patterns that always made rooms look so much bigger," says Jordan, who designed this chain-link variation suggestive of parking lots and playgrounds. Then he upholstered all his furniture with the fabric, used it for window treatments, and applied it to all the walls. The two-room apartment may be crowded, but now the pillows vanish into the couch and the couch blurs into the background. Behind a mahogany pedestal table that can seat four people in a pinch, the dining banquette tucked next to the fireplace is almost not there.

The diagonal line of the pattern helps deny the corners (and therefore the volume) of the rooms, expanding their dimensions. A handsome English Regency mahogany secretary performs a litany of duties, including that of desk, bar, and bookcase. "But the books tend to pile up,"

admits Jordan ruefully. "I stack them everywhere and just think of them as end tables."

Some visitors may wonder about his psychological health, murmuring about monomaniacal pattern and the ramifications of living inside a cage. "But I find this chain-link very liberating," says Jordan. "Of course, I think I'm outside the fence."

With one pattern on walls, windows, and upholstery in Greg Jordan's living room (opposite), furniture recedes rather than advances into space. An iron and glass coffee table is airy enough to encourage the flow. Chain-link fabric lines the walls of the bedroom (above) and takes a curtain call around the canopy bed. Overleaf: The fabric whisks even a wing chair into the background in the living room, where a thin black molding at the ceiling graphically jumps the fence.

color and PATTERN

If the walls are too close, the ceiling too low, the furniture too crowded—make them vanish. The results may be magical but the methods are not mysterious: simply pluck a few ideas from a design pro's portfolio of techniques.

One basic strategy, which comes in a hundred variations, is to dissolve the walls in strong pattern, bold color, or sheer gloss—stripes, florals, solids, enamels—so that edges cede to surface. A room becomes unhinged and loses its sense of boundary as soon as the floor, walls, and ceiling no longer meet in well-defined corners. Once these margins are denied, walls relinquish their sense of weight and volume and the room belongs to the furniture, which floats in the only thing left—space.

But sometimes it's more interesting to mask rather than erase. Screens and lattices are architecture's flirts, coyly allowing a tantalizing glimpse of the space beyond. Diaphanous fabrics draped over windows or canopy beds mist space and make boundaries indeterminate. Devices like screens and veils hold a room yet still allow space to seep through. The half-seen is more tantalizing than the full frontal picture.

For those who doubt that infinity is black, the proof is in this sitting room in an old Pennsylvania house decorated by Jeffrey Bilhuber, who turned out the lights to dramatically expand the space. Against this dark backdrop, objects—especially white objects—become detached and start to float. Bursting the bounds of gravity are twentieth-century design classics like the Alvar Aalto armchair and Isamu Noguchi rice-paper floor lantern (opposite). The long low shelf against the far wall—with a pale picture propped on top, rather than hung—accentuates the low horizon line. The black-painted walls bring out the sculptural character of an intimate grouping of nested game tables and bentwood chairs (above).

Color can be a lively distraction in a small room. Lavender cabinets (above) may not work in everyone's kitchen, but San Francisco designer Lou Ann Bauer tinted these to match a crazy-quilt backsplash of hand-sculpted tiles by Ann Sacks. Opposite: Operating on the Andy Warhol principle—if you're wearing a wig, dye it platinum blonde—New York architect Skip Boling painted his boxy kitchen bright coral and shocking pink. He punctured the walls with asymmetrical windows, skewing one and cantilevering a cracked-tile counter out the other to extend the space into a breakfast bar that can serve three.

"*My tendency is to simplify,*" says San Francisco architect Orlando Diaz-Azcuy, who whited out the redwood walls and red brick fireplace to expand his tiny 1940s clapboard cottage in Sonoma County. Since he's not fond of fancy curtains, he hung unobtrusive white canvas Roman shades at the windows. Inexpensive terra-cotta pots elevated on wrought-iron pedestals (above) become something special and establish another center of gravity to counterbalance the small-scale furniture. Versatile bamboo tables set up their own geometries, and are easily reconfigured to suit the occasion. The sofas flanking the fireplace (opposite) are slipcovered in white denim, and the similarly slipcovered armchairs move into the dining room for dinner.

Diaz-Azcuy uses the power of suggestion to make small rooms feel bigger. Taking his cue from one of Empress Josephine's fantasies at Malmaison, he painted all three bedrooms as trompe-l'oeil tents. The sophisticated visual illusion dematerializes the walls by implying the rooms are light, ephemeral structures temporarily pitched amid the trees. A vertical stripe always lifts the eye, and here it gives a graphic punch to the hallway (opposite). Wide French doors open the master bedroom (above) to the garden, heightening the breezy effect. A medley of moody blues—florals, plaids, checks, and geometrics, no two alike but all akin—smothers every available surface in Roger Banks-Pye's tiny London bedroom (overleaf). The late creative director of Colefax & Fowler tacked Indian crewelwork to the walls and glued a favorite chintz on the floor to emphasize surface rather than volume, spurning architecture in favor of atmosphere.

photo finish

No wonder Michael Berkowitz collects photography. Just walk into his two-room, 550-square-foot apartment on the parlor floor of a Federal row house in Manhattan's Greenwich Village and notice the power of black and white. "I love the graphic appeal of setting something dark against something light," says the men's clothing designer. "This may sound like I'm emotionally flawed, but after dealing with color all day, I couldn't come home to more of it."

Berkowitz's solution to color overload was to take a couple of gallons of white paint to the apartment's walls and ceilings, not to mention the doors, windows, cabinets, moldings, and the tongue-and-groove paneling in his bedroom. He wanted to unify the rooms and flood them with light at the same time; a monochromatic approach prevents small, detailed spaces like his from becoming fussy. Besides, more furnishings can fit within a neutralized shell. "Everything fell into place as if I'd always been collecting for this particular space," says the designer.

Into this chalky vessel Berkowitz poured the possessions of a lifetime spent looking closely in all sorts of places—from Sotheby's to swap meets—at all sorts of objects: old football megaphones, a miniature bark canoe, tramp art. A battered jelly cupboard stands next to a vintage split-reed couch and armchair worthy of an Adirondack camp. What these disparate treasures have in common is a certain sculptural quality. "It's not about nostalgia," says Berkowitz, contemplating his offbeat decor. "I don't think nostalgia is modern. This apartment is all about form."

Black-and-white photography sets the tone in Michael Berkowitz's diminutive apartment. Two vintage hand weights from a turn-of-the-century gym are poised, like sculpture, on the living room mantel (opposite). He brought home the majestic elk's antlers for the "drama of their form." The rustic split-reed furniture, though antique, had an intriguingly modern shape. A table behind the canvas-cushioned couch (above) does double duty as a bar.

A child's chair perched on the jelly cupboard (opposite) is not stranded there for lack of space. After Berkowitz bought it, he set it up there to examine it, liked the way it looked, and never took it down. A painted oar propped alongside the window was salvaged for its graceful shape. In the bedroom (above), a canvas-colored mattress is topped with a ticking featherbed, an Amish shawl, and a Shaker blanket—all set off with the graphic snap of a charcoal pillow, whose square shape also echoes the dark window shade.

in living color

T. Keller Donovan proves a master of spatial deceit in his own modest apartment. Born on the Fourth of July, the New York designer drapes the interiors in the colors of the American flag to mask the fact that the three rooms are small, dark, and unhandsome.

First, Donovan reinvented the architectural bones to stretch the space, as though dimensions were toffee. In a living room with measurements only a landlord could love, he made doorways taller by adding Georgian-style overdoors and cut down the mantel to raise the ceiling visually. "For someone as maniacal as me, the slightly off-center window posed a problem," he says. He deployed tall, white folding screens edged in red grosgrain ribbon to realign the opening and heighten the room—"that skinny red line takes your eye upward"—and angled the screeens toward the window in a forced perspective, which also creates the illusion of distance.

For New Yorkers born with the collecting gene who live in small spaces, objects can become a form of substance abuse. Donovan takes charge of the clutter by making it big, bold, and uniform: He treats his treasures graphically, arranging them in vibrant patterns of contrasting colors

that hopscotch blithely through the tight apartment.

Anything goes in the living room and foyer, as long as it is bright white or Diana Vreeland red. By starkly limiting his palette, the designer sets up a strategy for absorbing the red bowls, white pillows, red candlesticks, and white candles. The

Only the classical architectural shell is conservative in the living room of T. Keller Donovan's apartment (opposite). "My color sense was forged early on," he says. "I was dressed up in red, white, and blue every Fourth of July as a child." The brave red-and-white palette lends unexpected order to a space brimming with objects. In the foyer (above), a collection of framed engravings depicting heraldic medals gives the impression of a mullioned window in a room where there is none. The draped console underneath does triple duty as a desk, buffet, and hideaway for tools and paints.

mood turns blue in the kitchen, but the room maintains the same strategy of unifying an array of china and other objects with one consistent color combination: blue and white.

In the bedroom Donovan relents, letting white calmly take over, with accents of blue. Still he organizes by layering, with neatly framed architectural prints mounted on a wall of books over the bed. No one could ask for more reading material, but it doesn't have to look boring. These efficiently packed shelves become an architectural element in a room otherwise lacking such niceties. An even row of magazines at the top suggests the cornice of a fanciful facade in which the books are the bricks and the framed prints the windows.

Flanking the firecracker-red sofa in the living room (above), floor lamps with underscale shades inflate the volume of the sofa and add height to the room, giving an illusory assist to the elongated folding screens already pushing the ceiling. Dark blue paint camouflages the poor condition of the walls in the kitchen (right), where a mirror over the French bistro table expands the space. Collections of blue-and-white Spode china and African-inspired fabrics form a multicultural collage surrounding a counter crisply defined by a grouping of framed prints—"so I can look at something interesting while cooking," says Donovan. Overleaf: A wall of books serves as a backdrop for architectural prints in a room where the curtains and bed skirting portray a map of Mount Desert Island, Maine.

sleight OF HAND

Rooms expand when space flows, and space flows freely when the things that would stop it—solid walls, opaque fabrics, voluminous furniture—bow out of the picture. Transparency can make even a substantial object like a coffee table or a wall disappear. Raise high the roof beams—or even a bed, and let it stand on tall, spindly legs so that space passes underneath. Disembody a sofa by upholstering it in a shimmering silk that reflects the light, or choose see-through furniture like bentwood chairs and caned settees. Float shelves and cantilever tables so they appear suspended in thin air. Instead of breaking up a room with rugs, leave the floorboards bare, or create a continuous plane with wall-to-wall carpeting to accelerate the jet stream of space.

Stopping an interior wall short of a ceiling or a side wall allows the eye to peer from one room into another. Even a solid wall can become ambiguous with the right material. Frosted glass vaporizes boundaries and extends space by allowing shadowy views between rooms.

Of course, no space odyssey is complete without a deftly placed mirror. Reflections add another layer of intricacy. In the mind's eye, the square footage doubles. Space rebounds.

In a Manhattan penthouse, designer Ken Foreman denies the limits of space by whiting out the walls and then ignoring them by ushering all furniture to the center of the living room (opposite); there the pieces float on an island of carpet designed by Raymond Loewy. Lifted off the floor on short legs, the sofa and reading chair hover over their shadows, as a glass coffee table and wireframe chair designed by Harry Bertoia allow space to pass through unimpeded. Even the bookcase, supported on floor-to-ceiling poles, seems detached from the wall. A frosted glass door opens to the dining area (above), where a black console cantilevers daringly off the wall.

Mies   van   der   Rohe   is   famous   for   his   statement "Less is more," and in the bedroom of an apartment in one of Mies's Lakeshore Towers in Chicago, architect Robert D. Kleinschmidt rigorously applied this belief in an economy of means—which might be interpreted to mean that less furniture means more space. Kleinschmidt chose just a few good pieces, specifically a bed and a shelf that float above the floor (above), so space flows continuously beneath them. Without a doorsill between the bedroom and bath, the floor plane glides through seamlessly (opposite). So does the wall, where recessed cabinets allow the eye to slide between the two spaces. A translucent slice of sandblasted glass instead of the typical sheetrock wall further blurs the boundary between the two rooms.

Sliding translucent glass doors, like shoji screens, privatize individual rooms in a Manhattan loft designed by architect Michael Rubin (opposite). Pushed back, they open up a sweep of space, creating an enfilade from the bedroom through the dining area to the living room and inflating each with borrowed interior views. One more trick: The green interior wall doesn't meet the ceiling; instead, it's topped by clerestory glazing, which lets more space seep through. In a ranch house remodeled by San Francisco designer April Sheldon (above), see-through furniture is as porous as the cutout wall—with a wet bar behind the folding panels—that defines but does not separate living and dining areas. Overleaf: Even a small bedroom's boundaries evaporate when walls, floor, and windows are whited out. Against the pallor, Connecticut collector Dolph Leuthold's Thonet bentwood bed, floating at an angle, becomes a mere line drawing in space.

Leaning a mirror against the wall is "an optical illusion that expands space and reflects the light," says decorator Andrew Frank. The mahogany-framed mirror he designed for a Manhattan living room (opposite) dwarfs the other furniture and becomes a strong architectural element in an otherwise nondescript shell. Cool shades of beige clear the palette so the eye can focus on shape, from the bodiless stainless-steel plane of the coffee table to brass-trimmed ebony curves. A constantly shifting art collection is merely propped on the back of the sofa. The antique armoire in the bedroom (above) opens to reveal a computer workstation with a pullout desk.

screen saver

This vacation house on the Italian island of Sardinia is a long narrow rectangle only one room wide, but it feels like so much more because New York architects Kathryn Ogawa and Gilles Depardon exploited their entire repertoire of spatial tricks. Local restrictions and a limited budget kept the footprint down to 1,000 square feet, but the architects doubled the implied space by designing the house as a porous

pavilion, with a wall of French doors opening to a terrace facing the sea. Interior space flows across the threshold onto the terrace, which serves as an expansive outdoor room.

Inside, Ogawa and Depardon take their cue from the Japanese, who were masters at borrowing space. Instead of solid walls, wood lattice screens and sliding doors differentiate one long room into zones for cooking, dining, sitting, and sleeping. The graphic wood grid—repeated in large and small scale on windows, doors, shelves, shutters, and *brise-soleils*—becomes ornament and structure while still allowing space to flow between areas. "The rooms are all linked together rather than chopped apart," says Depardon. You can see straight through from one end of the house to the other, although a partition wall between the living and sleeping areas tactfully screens off the bed.

Sunlight streams through the thin membrane of glass and wood grids. Breezes waft through the French doors and open windows. Floored in stone and sparely furnished, this simple yet thoughtfully composed house is an indoor-outdoor platform for living in Sardinia's elements.

Architects Ogawa and Depardon designed the rooms of this vacation retreat to work together and extend into the landscape. A rear corridor (opposite) leading to a small bath and study expands with sliding glass corner doors at either end, opening onto two small rear terraces. Another terrace on the roof is accessible by an exterior staircase. When the wood shutters are raised, they form a sunscreen over the front terrace (above) facing the sea. The graphic wood grid provides a porous, weightless counterpoint to the thick white masonry walls and columns. Overleaf: Furniture in the living area is kept low and horizontal. Space seeps through perforated walls and wood screens. On either side of the Korean-made *tansu* chests, pocket doors can close off the bedroom.

A corner floor-to-ceiling window (opposite) breaks the wall and opens the bedroom to a side view. Traditional Japanese houses strongly influenced the facade, conceived as a thin, adaptable glass membrane layered with wood. The warm tones of the Douglas fir used throughout the house offset the white masonry walls. Wood slats over the doors (above) encourage breezes, and the sandwich of walls, doors, *brise-soleils*, and shutters forms a vertical and horizontal sunscreen that projects striations of shade. Built-in cupboards allow a mere modicum of furniture—a bed, chest, and an Isamu Noguchi paper lamp.

lost in space

The front door opens onto a narrow hallway sheathed in sea-green glass that glows. Like some otherworldly airlock, this entryway on the thirtieth floor of a Manhattan high-rise functions as a decompression chamber, a place to shed all the grit and agitation of the clamorous city before stepping into a serene retreat designed by Brian Stoner for a Japanese art collector.

In Stoner's hands, the bland box typical of recently constructed towers takes on an air of mystery and seems to magically expand. The designer invented a new geometry within the living room's basic square, dropping the edges of the ceiling into a swooping, amoebic curve. The variation in levels seems to stretch the room to a taller height, and creates a light cove that adds instant drama. The undulating circularity, echoed in the kidney-shaped couch and barrel chair, draws the eye from the floor-to-ceiling windows and reorients the focus within the room. Suddenly the newly introverted space has an identity beyond the

In a bland high-rise without architectural bones to preserve or volume to respect, why not dissolve the box? Brian Stoner turns a wall of windows in the living room (opposite) into a filmy scrim with sliding panels of translucent white silk. He updates the glamour of the vaguely Art Deco furniture with a hint of later eras. The antennae-like lamp behind the couch was copied from a 1950s design by Serge Mouille. The rhythmic mahogany screen is Stoner's homage to the streamlined modernism of French decorator Jean-Michel Frank. Reflective surfaces and fabrics deny the mass of the furniture. The entrance hall (above) is a luminous glass capsule, paved in limestone.

spectacular skyline view. In fact, Stoner prefers the visual quiet that prevails when the Japanese-style sliding panels of white silk are drawn to block out the cityscape.

Semitransparency adds depth to walls and finishes. Other materials were chosen according to the theory of reflectivity: the more luminous, the merrier. A lacquered coffee table sends back the light. Silver lamps don't even have to be turned on to create their own scintillating aura. The translucent silk curtains filter the light so that surfaces—pearl white leather, shagreen, soft wool felt, platinum leaf, and more of that ghostly sea-green glass—seem to shimmer. "I was trying to capture the texture and color of water," explains Stoner. "I matched the paint and the fabrics to the color of a full bathtub." The atmosphere is vaporous. Boundaries become indistinct and edges dissolve in the haze. Frosted glass squares perforate the doors. That rigorous symmetry contrasts with the curvaceous furniture, upholstered in plain, pale aqueous shades because Stoner saved all the pattern for the floor. The bold custom-made carpet grounds the room, and along with the dark mahogany pieces, keeps it from evaporating into the ether. The play of dark and light contributes to the cool enigmatic allure of this tranquil oasis high above the New York City streets.

The sinuous desk is finished in platinum leaf and white leather (above) to blend into the silvery monochromatic palette that prevails in the living room. A misty glass panel masks the radiator. The biomorphic black lacquer coffee table (opposite) fits into the curve of the kidney-shaped couch and echoes the undulating ceiling. Stoner mystifies the overhead light source by keeping it out of sight behind a cove. The result is a luminous glow, which further blurs the boundaries and expands space in this ethereal environment. Both the lamp and the end table have been platinum-leafed to practically dissolve in the light.

inventing
SPACE

Finding new space just means thinking about an old one in a different way. The discovery may be as obvious as climbing a wall—in other words, lifting the horizon of a room by hanging paintings nineteenth-century gallery style, one over the other up to the ceiling. Another overlooked spot hiding in plain sight is the middle of a room. Furniture usually hugs the walls, leaving the center unoccupied. Try a pedestal table piled with books in the middle of a living room, or usher the wallflowers toward the hub in conversational groups. Dramatic pieces like a canopy bed flourish on center stage, but this position is not for the self-effacing. Only distinguished items need apply. Any taken-for-granted territory is up for grabs. Consider closets and porches, or converting a two-car garage into a family room. More often, space is found in smaller quantities—a dormer window or a jog in a wall could be just large enough to accommodate a desk and chair for the person who craves a moment alone.

Those who invent space are often going against the grain of the floor plan, catching an opportunity normally cloaked by convention. Cultivate the unexpected and capitalize on the spontaneous—why not stow shoes under the sofa? Slip a slim storage cabinet behind a door, run shelves in a clean line above the windows, nest a bed under the eaves. Interrogate your square footage rather than merely accepting the givens.

The English are so good at picturesque clutter. Timothy Mawson, a Lancashire-born antiquarian book dealer transplanted to bucolic Connecticut, never saw a corner he could resist. A nook by the stairs in his nineteenth-century white clapboard house (opposite) is just big enough for a chair and a small table. Fellow Brit Barrie McIntyre, archivist for Colefax & Fowler, inhabits a Victorian row house in Kent, an ocean away. Operating on the principle that every recess is an opportunity, he shoehorned a chest of drawers into the niche that once held a kitchen range (above). Then he opened one drawer and set a piece of marbleized wood on top. The improvised buffet table in this kitchen turned dining room now serves drinks or dinner, overseen by a stuffed Barbary duck.

Being tucked into bed takes on a whole new context: From one loftlike upstairs room in their 1730 Hudson Valley farmhouse, the homeowners carved out a bath and three small bedrooms; a reproduction Dutch cupboard bed (opposite) saves space as it would once have conserved heat, with plenty of storage built in. Above: All you can see from the windows of this windswept beach house on Long Island Bay is water. Efficient as a berth on a boat, the loft bed was installed in a former bathroom. A chest of drawers hides behind the curtains. Even with rain splattering the window, this improvised guest bedroom offers a cozy port in a storm.

French home furnishings designer Julie Prisca leaves well enough almost alone in the attic of her half-timbered circa 1820 house in the Normandy countryside. In the summer, this space serves as an airy master bedroom, open to the bath at the other end. Swags of raw cotton, in the same color and configuration as the wishbone timbers, frame a seventeenth-century Dutch trompe-l'oeil bas-relief used as a headboard (above). Only a sunburst screen hand-painted by the designer hides the tub (opposite). A sinuous wrought-iron chair throws in a few curves under the triangular gable. Prisca also designed the metal, zinc, and wood washstand. The linear furniture lets space slide through and defers to the dramatic setting.

French philosopher Gaston Bachelard called the attic the dream space of a house, which makes it perfect for a study or bedroom. A canopy of twigs—actually wallpaper from Brunschwig & Fils—unifies the nooks and crannies of this long and narrow Manhattan attic study (opposite) designed by Katherine McCallum and Priscilla Ulmann. Awkward angles dissolve into the pattern. Bookcases are slipped under the sloping ceiling, and honey-toned furniture fits in comfortably. Above: In a bedroom where you can stand up only under the ridgepole, it made sense to set two undersize but cozy chairs. Scratch-coat plaster covers the walls and ceilings in the eighteenth-century Bucks County house, which designer Laura Bohn left plain and simple.

It is a truth universally acknowledged that no kitchen ever has enough space. Boston framer Roger Lussier can stand at the sink and reach back to close the folding doors in his compact kitchen (above). Pots hang from the ceiling to free up cupboards, and the microwave is squeezed in on a diagonal, with more storage above. Glass-fronted cabinets extend the space, almost like adding another window. Opposite: Four and a half inches was the depth of shelf architect William Ellis could fit into this unused kitchen corner. Shallow storage—just one can deep—lets him and his wife see everything at a glance, and hides the less attractive items behind doors. "It's my Mennonite Mondrian," he says. One horizontal merges into the windowsill. The top shelf continues over the window, offering room for expansion.

In a tall, slim house on one of those tight beachfront lots typical of southern California, Santa Monica architect Steven Ehrlich found space for a study simply by widening a second-floor landing (opposite). Low files add another surface, and the desk faces the ocean view. Above: San Francisco designer April Sheldon co-opted the garage in a 1950s ranch house, converting it into a two-car family room. The split-face concrete block on the new fireplace is her tongue-in-cheek play on stone. Secondhand furniture mixes in with her own inventions. But it's not 1958 anymore, so Sheldon took the modernist classic Eero Saarinen "Womb" chair and reupholstered it in a kaleidoscopic print. A media cabinet is more like a wall-size puzzle, made out of durable red Fin Ply (overleaf).

think big

"I'm not of the 'Darling, it's fabulous!' school," says decorator Celeste Cooper. Reason and ingenuity are behind every design move she makes. Her own Manhattan pied-à-terre, a small ground-floor apartment with no redeeming architectural features, has to function as both home and office (she splits her time between Boston and New York). "I believe in using all the space in a room," says the designer. In these 1,200 square feet, as systematized as a Ferrari dashboard, not one square inch is wasted. The bleached maple paneling in the living room masks touch-latch cabinets that open to reveal a pantry's worth of dishes behind one wall and her out-of-season wardrobe behind the other. Stereo equipment fills the dead space under a windowsill.

In a small room, Cooper's advice is simple: "Have fewer things, but make them larger. Use a sofa, even if it goes wall to wall, instead of a skimpy loveseat. Forget all those fussy little end tables—just do a large coffee table. I like one big surface, with room for books, magazines, and drinks."

Instead of jamming her living room sofa up against the wall, Cooper pulled it out and put a linen-covered table

To get the most out of a small room, follow Celeste Cooper's instructions: "Limit your palette." In her own living room (opposite), she chose taupe. "Hang curtains from the ceiling or the bottom of crown moldings; otherwise the room looks stunted." The designer, not a fan of traditional drapery hardware or fabric, used the Blome system of stainless steel cable and clips to hang menswear material. Since it's a street-level apartment, the shades pull in both directions. Vetoing conventional wisdom, she painted the same shade on walls and ceiling and used high gloss overhead to reflect more light. Answering her own question, "Why should books always be upright?" Cooper designed two towers of shelves (above), perfect for oversize art tomes.

behind it, providing a place for a reading lamp and accessories (plus Christmas ornaments, wallpaper rolls, and bolts of fabric, stored underneath). "Placing a table behind the sofa creates the illusion of more depth in a small space," she explains. "Besides, I like some breathing room around a piece of furniture. The space you leave empty is as important as the space you fill."

Each room is set up to perform multiple functions. The office—tucked behind a partition wall on the way to the kitchen—becomes a guest room, thanks to the bed-size banquette under the window. The dining room morphs into a conference room so clients can pore over blueprints spread out on the table. The tiny bedroom is a triumph of imagination over reality. "Frankly, I sleep in a walk-in closet," says Cooper, who draped all the walls with creamy cotton and smuggled in shelves and racks of clothing behind the fabric. No one stepping into the room would guess that a television set lurks behind those romantic curtains.

The secret in a small space is combining discipline with indulgence. "Chanel once said you should get all dressed up with your jewelry on, then look in the mirror and take one thing off," explains Cooper. "Design is a comparable editing process." Each of her rooms is pared down and programmed to suit her particular requirements. The small apartment functions efficiently, yet still feels luxurious. "That's compulsory," says Cooper. "Beauty doesn't have to be dumb."

"I don't care if something is antique or not," says Cooper. "What counts is presence, not provenance." A wrought-iron console table found at a flea market offers an object lesson (above). On the other side of the partition wall is the designer's office (opposite), with a wall-size bulletin board made of 4 by 8-foot sheets of corkboard painted the same cream as the walls. "Organize and containerize," advises Cooper. Repetition is the key to orderly storage. A wall of linen-covered boxes and wire bins holds a slew of samples within arm's reach of her desk.

Cooper never misses a storage opportunity. The tiny bedroom is literally a walk-in closet: Behind the curtains cocooning the room she stashes clothing and accessories (above left). The limited palette also applies to her wardrobe, which is basically black and taupe (above right). "I could get dressed in the dark if I had to, since everything goes together," she says. Even her shoes are stacked in file boxes. A mirror hung over the fabric (opposite) inflates the space. But Cooper was not afraid to make a small room even smaller with the encompassing curtains and closets. "Amateurs might try to camouflage the smallness. Instead, I emphasized it to create an intimate, dramatic room."

double DUTY

Perhaps for the happy few, space is no object and rooms are dedicated to individual activities. But for most of us today, a separate breakfast room, sewing room, sunroom, and family room are more likely to be found on a *Clue* gameboard. Now that living space has shrunk, strategy—not square footage—plays the leading role in accommodating a household. One solution lies in designing spaces that lead multiple lives. In a one-room apartment, furniture can be organized into zones for eating, working, and sleeping. Task lights over certain areas can create invisible walls. In slightly larger quarters, the dining room can sleep guests on banquettes, or function as a library with the addition of bookshelves.

Movable furniture—small tables that roll together to form a long one, chairs that do double duty for working and dining—compounds the possibilities. Sometimes even the architecture slides. Japanese houses offer an inspired example of small spaces that take on multiple configurations, with shoji screens running every which way. If putting a wall on tracks can't be arranged, nothing beats a folding screen for flexibility and allure on a tight spatial budget.

Unlike most mere mortals, designer Albert Hadley is not pining for more space. He has lived in the same modest three-room apartment for twenty years. One reason it works so well is versatility. His dining room moonlights as a guest room (opposite). His signature red sparks up the reading lamps and the daybed's lacquered base. The mirrored alcove's dimensions are neatly replicated by corkboard (above) painted cerulean blue and big enough to tack up blueprints or sketches, allowing the room to serve as his study as well. Bored with plain ceilings, the designer painted this one dark, making it disappear.

Designer Tom Scheerer decided to accentuate the positive—13-foot ceilings—and make the most of the negative in this 17 by 18-foot studio. Bookshelves (above), which look even taller since they're narrow, stretch straight to the sky. A mirrored coffee table disappears into the wall-to-wall sisal, which creates a continuous floor plane rather than mincing the room up with rugs.

Floor-to-ceiling mirror flanks the fireplace (above right) to imply space beyond the chimney wall. "The illusion is ruined if you see yourself," says Scheerer, explaining why he didn't continue the mirror above the mantel. He kept the upholstered furniture low and made sure the other pieces were more open—like the bentwood chairs and the thin plane of the dining table/desk.

In a long narrow room difficult to furnish Virginia Witbeck designed two graceful low-lying chaises for either side of the fireplace (opposite). "The room would be too chopped up with two flanking sofas, and just one facing the fireplace would mean turning your back on the view," says the designer, who opened up the rear wall with five French doors leading to the garden. A Queen Anne dropleaf table (above) transforms the living room into a dining room; the dining chairs stand eighteenth-century-style against the walls. A tower of stacking tables and twin tray tables move around as needed, and the Anglo-Indian tea table in front of the fireplace is just the right size for an intimate champagne supper. Black-and-white upholstery allows Witbeck to change the color scheme just by tossing on some new throw pillows. Practicality marries elegance in the curtains, bordered with black where they brush the floor.

Guests can now roost in this former chicken coop since designer Michael Stanley added windows, a fireplace, and a Pullman kitchen. Blue-and-white gingham upholsters all the furniture (opposite and above), and this palette pulls together zones for cooking, dining, and late-night chats. Overleaf: In a Manhattan living room by Kathryn Ogawa and Gilles Depardon, geometric tables made from planes of pure ash supported by waxed steel squares come together to form one big dining table. The sofa near the window folds out into a guest bed and can be enclosed by the undulating linen curtain for privacy. Suspended from a ceiling track by copper wire, the spectral curtain, open at both top and bottom, lets in the light while masking an unfortunate view.

Desks for designers like Christian Liaigre, who quiets rooms visually by taking away "the small, superficial things," present a particular problem: what to do with the clutter? In a duplex apartment in Paris, Liaigre preserved his characteristically clean lines and bold geometries. At one end of a sparsely furnished dining room, he merged Ming Dynasty and sleek Modernism to create an armoire so large it blends into the wall, yet so shallow it doesn't invade the space. With the doors open, the dining room metamorphoses into a study, focused on an indirectly lit desk that pulls down from the bookshelves.

living it up

When interior designer Sara Bengur stepped into the elegant drawing room of a Greenwich Village townhouse, her eyes went up: The space, already organized with a bath and kitchen located beneath a sleeping deck, was small, but the ceiling soared—fifteen feet, to be exact. In Manhattan, space—especially vertical space—is the ultimate luxury, and Bengur was convinced she and her husband would be happy in this former drawing room, even if it measured a mere 700 square feet. "Europeans manage to live graciously in only one room, and I decided to try and re-create that Old World salon atmosphere," she explains.

Color would play a major role. "My background is Turkish, and I love warm Mediterranean colors like ocher, apricot, terra cotta, and brown." She chose fabrics within that palette, instead of breaking up her one great room with different hues. To enhance the impression of height, furniture was kept low to the ground. Tall bookcases, which would have enclosed the space, were banished.

The apartment's window treatments are deliberately simple, so they don't cover up the well-bred moldings

Sara Bengur resolved that nothing would diminish the height of the ceilings in her apartment, so she kept a low horizon line of furniture in her one great room (opposite). By choosing a fabric for the Roman shades that matches the wall color, she creates a sense of continuous flow. Indonesian ottomans and a small Jean-Michel Frank sofa mix comfortably with family heirlooms: The Queen Anne chair upholstered in apricot raw silk and the Gothic Kittinger chair came with her husband. The neoclassical demi-lune coffee table (above) picks up the curve of the arch overhead. Luckily it has pullout leaves, to hold even more books.

painted creamy white. White also highlights the dramatic arch that spans the room and shelters the sleeping loft, where the mattress sits directly on the floor to take advantage of every bit of height. A vintage Italian screen painted in soft grays suggests a view where there is none, as well as concealing the entrance to the kitchen and bathroom.

Defining the room in formal terms doesn't mean Bengur can't mix in a touch of surrealism, via her art collection. And the Swedish chairs around the dining table-cum-desk are contemporary, made up of individual dowels set into S-curved frames. But the piece that means the most to her is the Tabriz rug that has been in her family since her father was a baby. When it fit perfectly in the room, Bengur knew she was home.

The dining table is an old farm table (opposite) draped in a French linen sheet. For a big party it gets pushed farther back and becomes a buffet. Books that would normally fill the banished bookcases march wittily up the stairs to the sleeping loft. Under the graceful arch, Bengur playfully mixes scale with gilded night tables looming over the low-lying bed (above). Some pictures hang on the walls and others are propped on the floor. Two chandeliers decked with real candles perch, unexpectedly, at toe level.

GREAT SPACE

five ingenious solutions

going
SKY HIGH

When you trust the weather, anything can go, even the walls. With the sun a dependable fixture more than 300 days a year, the Santa Barbara climate encouraged architectural designer Arn Ginsburg to ring his one-bedroom, 1,100-square-foot apartment around a square courtyard and then open the walls to the open air. None of the interior rooms are large, but integrating the broad outdoor space into the floor plan inflates their apparent size.

"This is not a new idea," says Ginsburg. "The Greeks and Romans built atrium houses. But what really makes this space feel expansive is the way I 'dissolved' the walls." He creates that illusion with accordion-like interior walls that ride on tracks and vanish into closets, so that when the house is fully opened, space extends from one exterior wall to the other. Ordinary glass walls just wouldn't do the trick: Sitting inside and looking out through glass is very different from being able to dance through space.

By using the same indoor-outdoor carpet everywhere and treating both interior and exterior walls as clean, crisp planes, Ginsburg equates the two kinds of space; minimizing

The sky's the limit in this apartment, one of four similar units in a building designed by Arn Ginsburg. The rooms are arranged around a central courtyard. When the folding interior doors are open, the living room (opposite) and bedroom flanking the open courtyard become one expansive space. Ginsburg keeps his environmental pleasures simple; the dramatic but understated interiors play a supporting role to the main character, the courtyard, which delivers the sky, sun, and elements. Above: In this view from the courtyard looking out, a simple black awning marks the entrance to the apartment.

the difference between inside and out facilitates the flow. "I walk into friends' houses three times the size of mine that don't feel half as expansive," he says. "It's as simple as numbers: 16½ by 44 feet. That's the size of my space when the folding doors are open. Now how many houses offer a room that big that still feels completely private?"

Ginsburg could pack a lot into this kind of space, but instead he chooses to live very minimally. "I don't own a lot, and that's a big advantage. All I need is fresh air and daylight." No clutter clouds these corners. "I love the emptiness," he explains. "This way, I always feel as if I have enough room." When he walks through the front door, serenity takes over. And there was one totally unexpected side effect to living right under the sky. "I learned how many different birds there are," says Ginsburg. "Every few minutes, another one flies over, and I hear birdsong all day long."

The accordian-like interior doors open to the living room (opposite), which also serves as dining room and office. The Arne Jacobsen "Ant" chairs around the table provide a jolt of color in an otherwise undecorated space. "There are no pictures to draw attention to the walls, so you don't have a clear idea where they stop and start," says Ginsburg. "That stretches the space." Above: A window directly across the courtyard from the entrance punctures the exterior wall and dissolves still another boundary.

A simple, efficient service corridor runs like a spine along the back of the apartment. Pale wood and gleaming metal catch the light in the galley kitchen (opposite). The bathroom mirror (above left) goes all the way up into the skylight shaft and continues down under the sink, which makes a tight space feel bigger. A separate tub behind the bedroom can be closed off (above right). Overleaf: The black-sheeted bed is poised in the middle of the bedroom, and the table across the courtyard can rise or fall depending on the configuration of the supporting pedestals. "Everything floats in this apartment," says Ginsburg. "Nothing touches the walls."

down to EARTH

No point in pretending. "It's teensy," Mallory Marshall says bluntly, describing her turn-of-the-century white clapboard guest cottage a stone's throw from the water on Islesboro Island, Maine. "It's just enough room for two people who are falling in love or four really good friends. We had six people stay once and they never spoke to each other again."

This wife, mother, and decorator has very definite ideas about living contentedly in a small space. Keep it simple is the first rule. "Outside on the coast of Maine there's so much color, which is one reason why all those artists have come here to paint." Instead of trying to compete with the view, her rooms just frame it in pure salt white, accented with neutral tones of sea green to give the eye a rest.

Some potential guests may find her next decision shocking: She turned one bedroom into a bathroom. "In a very small space, it's better to have more baths and fewer bedrooms," she explains. This house offers two bathtubs and an outdoor shower, plus a small footbath suitable for dogs and children. "Just think of the inside baths as a refuge, and the outdoor baths as repositories of filth."

Simplicity rules the waves in Mallory Marshall's cottage. A doorless cabinet holds plates in the tiny dining room (opposite), which was improvised from a porch. White floors, white walls, and white ceilings stretch the boundaries of the space. The turn-of-the-century house offers lots of useful nooks and crannies, like this corner of the kitchen (above), populated with flea market finds. Overleaf: In the living room, over-the-window shelves hold pinecones and rainy-day paperbacks. The loveseat-size couch doesn't overwhelm the space, and like most of the furniture, it's conveniently set on wheels.

There isn't a lot of fluff and ruffle in the two cozy bedrooms, just exactly what's needed—no more, no less. According to the Marshall doctrine, that means "a dresser with three drawers—one each for pants, shirts and underwear. Two small drawers on top for rubber bands, lost buttons, and fishhooks. One light cotton blanket and a comforter for cold nights (there's also a basket of socks under each bed). Two hooks on the wall for wet things. One vase for just-picked wildflowers, a stick to keep the window open, a box of thumbtacks to put up wet watercolors, candles and matches in case of a storm, and a stash of forbidden candy bars for sweet dreams."

Most items have multiple personalities. Blankets migrate out to the grass for picnics. A kitchen stool becomes a high chair. "In a small house, the living room is a place where you actually live," says Marshall. "If it rains, you've got to have two comfortable chairs and a table big enough for a jigsaw puzzle." When the paraphernalia of daily life has been pared down to the essentials, each object takes on a new significance. "Guests get attached to their particular cracked cup," says Marshall. "Most of us are choking on objects. We all live with too many things that require too many choices. In this small cottage, you choose once, and that's it."

One corner of the sleeping porch (above) is just wide enough for an Empire-style rocking chair, which no summer house should be without. Repainting the floor is the children's project every spring. This year they cut cardboard into a comb and swirled in whirlpools and waves. Nobody ever reads *The Wall Street Journal* (more likely Nancy Drew) on the nineteenth-century iron daybed (opposite) at the other end of the room. Anyone missing in the afternoon can usually be found here, napping, and it conveniently accommodates overflow guests. There's also an open-air porch outside with a hanging cradle.

A V i c t o r i a n   d r e s s e r   a n d   m i r r o r take on a whole new personality in this bedroom (opposite). White linen curtains filter Maine's crystalline light in most rooms—"They're like sails for the house," says Marshall, who sometimes sews mussel shells onto the hem to keep them from billowing all over. "Plus I can literally hose them down, hang them on the line and let them blow dry." There's not much wall space under the eaves in the bathroom. Maps tacked onto the sloping ceiling allow guests to plan the next day's outing while soaking in the tub (above left); a see-through rattan chair barely interrupts the vista of white in the airy room (above right).

mirror, MIRROR

No smoke, just mirrors—that was all architect John Marsh Davis needed to make his own 980-square-foot Sausalito house overlooking bobbing sailboats feel at least twice the size. Guests may come for dinner and linger over coffee and still fail to realize that the room they are sitting in does not keep on going beyond the fireplace. What looks like continuous space to the left of the chimneypiece is just one of many strategically placed mirrors. People often walk over to see for themselves, touching the glass and then turning to the architect-cum-magician for more clues to the spatial prestidigitation. What else is actually mirror?

Just above, where it looks like space flows right through the house under the rafters, is another mirror. And the skylights, which break open the box and seem to merge effortlessly into French doors out to the balcony—those first panes of glass above the cornice line are actually a reflection in a long, angled mirror. The sum total of all these illusions augments the sense of the existing square footage to such an

To make his 1908 Shingle-style cottage look much larger than its square footage, architect John Marsh Davis seems to pull space out of a hat. One big room shoots up with a column of books (opposite), then stretches sideways through French doors. In a sleight-of-hand gesture that lets space seep through, the bookcase—which separates living and dining areas and also camouflages a necessary support—doesn't meet the ceiling all the way across. A mirror dissolves the wall beyond the French doors. "The trick with mirrors is to put them where they reflect the architecture, not yourself," says Davis. The woodwork around the falcon painting (above) meets the muntin on the front door with an interlocking complexity worthy of Mondrian. Another mirrored wall behind the vase of peonies brings more greenery indoors.

extent that when Davis describes the house as basically one room with a few partitions, it's hard to believe him. Zones for cooking, dining, sitting, and sleeping are thoughtfully laid out within the handsome shell. This layered composition of finely wrought woodwork delineates each section of the house while keeping all areas open to one another. As a result, the architect simultaneously achieves the intimacy of a small space and the impact of a large one.

The mirror ruse is just one clever bluff in this self-aggrandizing structure. Davis also learned a few spatial tricks from Frank Lloyd Wright, including the notion that walls need not be continuous, or even solid, allowing one area to borrow space from another. "Wright's houses open to the landscape yet still have a sheltered feeling and a warmth about them," says Davis. "He was a profound influence that I've never outgrown."

Davis's home reflects a masterful command of voids and solids to conjure up a sense of infinite space. This structure is more frame than wall, porous rather than solidly impenetrable to light and air. No ceiling blocks the soaring rafters, and skylights lighten the visual weight of the roof. Space flows through the house and out to the bougainvillea-draped garden. This one versatile room dilates and expands, defying its own dimensions.

Diners at the round table (left) with a view of Richardson Bay sit in reproduction Frank Lloyd Wright barrel chairs, which share an Arts & Crafts sensibility with the interior woodwork. The trusses are dramatic, not functional, but they add movement and energy to the space and suggest a bridge, or a span of the Eiffel Tower. Opposite: A Japanese-like wood grille softens the impact of the California sun through the skylight, which seems to fuse into the French doors. But that bottom row of panes is just an optical illusion, reflected in a mirror pitched at a 90-degree angle above the cornice. A Japanese paper lantern is a buoyant touch, floating above the sisal floor.

A m i r r o r e d w a l l t o t h e l e f t o f t h e f i r e p l a c e (opposite) does a
disappearing act. The abstract gray rectangles conceal a crack from a recent earthquake.
Triangular mirrors above the cornice line on both sides of the chimneypiece reflect the rafters
and create the illusion that space flows through, but in reality the bedroom beyond has a flat ceiling.
A pocket door to the right of the fireplace pulls out to close off this sleeping area. The windows
directly behind the fireplace (above) are hung with small-scale copies of Frank Lloyd Wright's
stained glass from the Coonley Playhouse. The bed is out of sight on the left. Shallow drawers
in the dressing area mean Davis doesn't have to dig to find a pair of socks.

Everything is shipshape in the galley kitchen (above). A window turns the corner seamlessly—thanks to mitered glass, which breaks the sense of the wall as boundary. Stools tuck under a compact breakfast bar, and pots hang within reach of the commercial stove. Opposite: Adjacent to the house, Davis's office is only eight feet wide. But mirrors line the long walls and magnify the compact volume. Skylights turn the room into a greenhouse, and geraniums, bougainvillea, and an orange tree bring the garden indoors.

cram COURSE

If only Alexander the Great, Napoleon, and Attila the Hun had consulted Miles Redd first, they might have understood a very basic principle about space—that it's possible to expand by implosion. "The more you cram into a room, the bigger it seems," says Redd, a decorator with an addictive penchant for flea markets, thrift shops, and local trash heaps.

Redd occupies a minuscule apartment in New York City's East Village with a room count of three on a good-hair day. But he did not let its size dampen his spirit or diminish his spatial aspirations: Redd is a conqueror; the world is his oyster; everything is game.

Redd made room by employing several strategies simultaneously. He layered, he elevated, he stacked—and then he threw in some mirrors. Every horizontal surface in this apartment bristles with whatnots—even the walls get similar treatment (witness a wreath atop a six-over-six mirror atop molding). Utilizing every bit of space, he hangs a black-and-white photograph in a silver frame on a door and mounts two oval portraits on a window. His empire of objects is vertical as well as horizontal: vases crown columns

"I'm a compulsive shopper," confesses Miles Redd, and the resulting profusion invades his apartment and obliterates walls, floors, and ceilings. Moody black-and-white photographs populate the tiny bedroom (opposite). A vintage airplane photograph (above) strafes a jaunty bowler hat. Assorted mirrors in the living room (overleaf) double the plethora of objects. The eye never stops in a space animated by the visual staccato of dozens of small and large things. The minutiae expand the room and take the mind off its real dimensions—and the fact that his shoes are stowed under the fire engine–red couch.

and towers of books. There is no glass ceiling here: Redd uses the full height of the apartment, pushing the envelope with rows of drawings and airplane photographs, five high, no problem. The bedroom also functions as library and den, with the bed suspended overhead on chains. The living room serves as a closet, dining room, and office. The bathtub resides in the kitchen. Even the floor is busy, painted in a green-and-white harlequin pattern; the use of the diagonal expands the space visually (or would, if you could see more of it beneath the clutter). "Sometimes I feel I'm just storing these things until I move to a larger place, where I'll eventually pare down," muses the designer. "Meantime, in my mind all this stuff makes this tenement look romantic. It's a pastiche of glamour—my little Alphabet City Versailles."

When the lid is down the bathtub in the kitchen (above left) doubles as a chopping block. The bedroom dresser supports a not-so-still life (above right). The symmetry of paired lamps and wall brackets around a gilded mirror is quickly overwhelmed by the exuberance of assorted photos and flower arrangements. Opposite: The futon for television-watching is set against striped walls and a silver-paper–gridded closet. Redd has yet to fall off the suspended bed, reachable by ladder. "It's very cozy up there, like being rocked in a cradle," he says.

cinderella STORY

The client had only one request. "Make it beautiful," he told Sausalito designer Stephen Shubel. In the best fairy godmother tradition, Shubel waved his measuring tape and paintbrush and put the homely 1920s clapboard cottage behind the white picket fence through a Cinderella transformation. Now this Sonoma, California, house with a pool out back looks far grander than a modest 950 square feet.

"Small rooms seem more spacious if you use fewer colors," says the designer, who picked ice white and periwinkle blue to keep the house cool in summer and carried them throughout the main rooms. Others might choose dainty furniture for small spaces, but Shubel operates on the opposite theory. "I think you should put overscale furniture in rooms like these," he explains. "Big pieces fool your eye into thinking a space is larger." In the living room, he had the sofa and chairs custom-made to get just the right heft, then covered them in blue and white oxford cloth to blend into the walls. "There is nothing more space-expanding than using the same fabric for the upholstery and curtains," he says. "It definitely stretches a room."

"This room is the size of an area rug," says designer Stephen Shubel, who recast a 9 by 11-foot sitting room as a tented fantasy adorned with a tortoiseshell sunburst mirror (opposite) to distract attention from its cramped proportions. The illusion was so appealing that the client now sleeps there, on a daybed facing French doors that open to the backyard pool (above). To the left is the garage-turned-guest house, which adds another 300 square feet of usable charm to the yellow clapboard cottage. House and guest house combine with the paved deck to shape the backyard into an outdoor room.

Dull dowager brown furniture got a facelift of refreshing white paint, but the most dramatic transformation occurred in the only room in the house that opens to the pool, a minuscule 9 by 11-foot area awkwardly broken up by five separate doors. Shubel decided to pull out all the stops. Daydreaming of beach cabanas on the French Riviera, he concocted fanciful curtains complete with a serrated valance trimmed with tassels and ran them all around the room. By changing the subject so completely, no one even noticed the paltry dimensions anymore. The sitting room became so romantic that the client appropriated it for his own bedroom. He just pulls a panel aside to go through one of the masked doorways, and the periwinkle blue fabric beautifully frames the view of the pool.

A blue-and-white palette homogenizes walls and furniture in the main rooms. The living room's big square ottoman (above) does double duty as a coffee table and as extra seating space. Shubel painted both the red brick fireplace and the desk tucked to one side white, then took his brush to the reproduction cane-backed Louis XVI chairs in the dining room (opposite). Others might flinch at painting an Edwardian mahogany dining table white, but Shubel did it, for continuity's sake. In fact, since the client wanted a durable surface, impervious to chilled drinks, he actually had it lacquered by an auto-body shop. A chalky Venetian glass chandelier hangs above, and curtain rods placed high above the windows visually lift the low ceilings.

White paint reconciles different vintages of furniture. The orange sherbet paint on the guest room walls (opposite) is a nice break from all the blue. Drifting mosquito-net tents are practical and lend height and interest to a restful room with no art on the walls. Shubel added sheetrock walls to the former garage (above) and painted them pink. Rather than capping the room with a ceiling, he took advantage of all the height and accentuated the beams with white paint. French doors open the guest house to the pool. Anticipating wet bathing suits, the designer made the wicker chair cushions, the bedspread, and even the curtains out of white terrycloth.

design DIRECTORY

Lou Ann Bauer
Bauer Interior Design
San Francisco, California

Sara Bengur
New York, New York

Jeffrey Bilhuber
Bilhuber Inc.
New York, New York

Sam Blount
Sam Blount Inc.
New York, New York

Laura Bohn
Laura Bohn Design Associates
New York, New York

Skip Boling
New York, New York

Nancy Braithwaite
Nancy Braithwaite Interiors, Inc.
Atlanta, Georgia

Gregory D. Cann
Cann + Company
Boston, Massachusetts

Walter Chatham
Walter Chatham Architect
New York, New York

Celeste Cooper
Repertoire
New York, New York
Boston, Massachusetts

John Marsh Davis
Sausalito, California

Gilles Depardon and Kathryn Ogawa
Ogawa/Depardon
New York, New York

Orlando Diaz-Azcuy
Orlando Diaz-Azcuy Designs
San Francisco, California

T. Keller Donovan
New York, New York

Steven Ehrlich
Steven Ehrlich Architects
Santa Monica, California

William Ellis
New York, New York

Tricia Foley
New York, New York

Ken Foreman
Ken Foreman Designs and Interiors
New York, New York

Andrew Frank
Andrew Frank Interior Design
New York, New York

Arn Ginsburg
Santa Barbara, California

Albert Hadley
Parish-Hadley Associates, Inc.
New York, New York

Carlos Jimenez
Carlos Jimenez Architectural
    Design Studio
Houston, Texas

Greg Jordan
Greg Jordan Incorporated
New York, New York

Robert D. Kleinschmidt
Powell/Kleinschmidt
Chicago, Illinois

Sheila Camera Kotur
New York, New York

Christian Liaigre
Liaigre Design Co.
Paris, France
(in the U.S. through Holly Hunt Ltd.,
    New York, New York)

James Lumsden
Los Angeles, California

Mallory Marshall
Mallory James Interiors
Portland, Maine

Katherine McCallum
McMillen
New York, New York

Miles Redd
New York, New York

Michael Rubin
Michael Rubin, Architects
New York, New York

Tom Scheerer
Charleston, South Carolina

April Sheldon
April Sheldon Design
San Francisco, California

Stephen Shubel
Sausalito, California

Charles Spada
Charles Spada Interiors
Boston, Massachusetts

Michael C. Stanley
Putnam, Connecticut

Brian Stoner
Brian Stoner & Associates
New York, New York

Priscilla Ulmann
Parish-Hadley Associates, Inc.
New York, New York

Tom Vanderbeck
T. Vanderbeck Antiques and Interiors
Hadlyme, Connecticut

Virginia Witbeck
Bridgehampton, New York

Peter Wheeler
Boston, Massachusetts

Vicente Wolf
New York, New York

photography CREDITS

1	William Waldron	86-87	Peter Margonelli
2	Eric Roth	88-93	Antoine Bootz
5	Langdon Clay	94-97	William Waldron
6	William Waldron	98	Richard Felber
8	William Waldron	99	Michael Dunne
10	Eric Roth	100	Kari Haavisto
12	Jon Jensen	101	Lizzie Himmel
13	Scott Frances	102-103	Laura Resen
14-17	Tim Street-Porter	104	Thibault Jeanson
18	Jeff McNamara	105	Jeff McNamara
19	Eric Roth	106	Thibault Jeanson
20	Jack Winston	107	Tom McWilliam
21	Antoine Bootz	108	Tim Street-Porter
22	Eric Roth	109-111	Jeremy Samuelson
23-25	Richard Felber	112-117	Peter Margonelli
26-31	Oberto Gili	118-119	Pieter Estersohn
32-37	Thibault Jeanson	120-121	Kari Haavisto
38	Jeff McNamara	122-123	Erica Lennard
39	Oberto Gili	124-125	Richard Felber
40-41	Peter Margonelli	126-127	David Richmond
42	Thibault Jeanson	128-129	Jacques Dirand
43	William Waldron	130-133	Alec Hemer
44-45	Richard Felber	134-143	Grey Crawford
46-53	Scott Frances	144-151	William Waldron
54-57	Tom McWilliam	152-159	Jon Jensen
58-59	William Waldron	160-165	Oberto Gili
60-61	Mark Darley	166-171	Tom Eckerle
62-65	Jeremy Samuelson	174	David Phelps
66-67	Jacques Dirand	176	Thibault Jeanson
68-71	Thibault Jeanson		
72-77	Scott Frances		
78-79	Peter Margonelli		
80-81	Scott Frances		
82	Judith Watts		
83	Jeremy Samuelson		
84-85	Catherine Leuthold		

INDEX

Balance
    editing for, 11, 39, 114
    elegant, 39, 40–41
    simplicity and, 46, 47–53
Bathrooms, 141, 145, 151
    simply neutral, 36, 37
    storage in, 103
    translucent wall in, 80, 81
Beds
    bunk, 13
    canopy, 20, 21
    Dutch cupboard, 100, 101
    faux canopy, 18, 19
    as focal points, 20, 21, 83, 84–85
    indoor/outdoor, 136, 137, 141, 142–143
    loft, 101
    mosquito-netted, 36, 170, 171
    suspended, 164, 165
    wall-to-wall, 36
Bookshelves. See Shelving
Boundaries
    dissolving, 58, 59, 78, 79, 80–85, 137
    translucent, 80, 81, 82, 83
    walls without, 136, 137–143
    whiting out, 13, 83, 84–85
Color
    beige, 112, 113–117
    black/white, 68, 69–71
    bold, 26, 27–31, 58, 59, 60, 61
    cool gray, elegant, 39, 40–41
    defining rooms, 48–49, 50–51
    for illusion, 11, 13
    limiting, 113, 167
    objects floating in, 58, 59, 78, 79
    red, white & blue, 72, 73–77
    removing boundaries with, 58, 59, 118, 119
    silvery flow of, 94, 95–97
    subtle, soothing, 32, 33–37
    unifying effect of, 166, 167–171
    warm Mediterranean, 130, 131–133
    white shades, 32, 33–37
Double duty rooms, 119–133
    dining rooms, 114, 118, 119, 122, 123, 128
    folding screens for, 119
    furniture for, 119, 125
    guest rooms, 114, 125, 126–127
    kitchens, 164
    living rooms, 122, 123, 125, 126–127, 138, 139
    offices, 114, 128, 129, 138, 139
    strategies for, 119
    studios, 120–121, 130, 131–133
Editing possessions, 11, 39, 114
Fabrics
    blending rooms with, 54, 55–57, 166, 167
    bright, dramatic, 30
    warm-colored, 130, 131
Furniture
    ample, cozy, 14–17
    armoires, 87, 128, 129
    Art Deco-inspired, 94, 95–97
    blending rooms with, 54, 55–57
    in boundless room, 58, 59
    defining space, 48–49, 50–51
    double duty, 119, 125, 126
    floating, 48–49, 58, 59, 78, 79, 80, 141
    floral upholstered, 44, 45
    geometric, 125, 126–127
    hiding workspace, 87

informal eclectic, 28, 29, 30, 31
    low, horizontal, 89, 90–91, 121, 130, 131
    movable, 119, 145, 146–147
    overscale, 112, 113, 128, 129, 166, 167
    secondhand, 109, 110–111
    see-through, 83
    underscale, 13, 62, 63, 105
High ceilings, 120–121, 130, 131–133
Illusion
    canopy bed, 18, 19
    color and, 11, 13
    editing for, 11, 39, 114
    with mirrors, 121, 153
    pattern and, 11, 54, 55–57
    pictures for, 12, 13
    Provençal color fest, 26, 27–31
    trompe-l'oeil, 18, 64, 65
Ingenious solutions
    Arts & Crafts mirror magic, 152, 153–159
    California homes, 152, 153–159, 166, 167–171
    Maine cottage, 144, 145–151
    open-air apartment, 136, 137–143
    petit apartment, 160, 161–165
Inventing space, 99–117
    in attics, 102, 103, 104, 105
    for big things, 112, 113–117
    for cozy bedrooms, 100, 101, 102, 103, 105, 116, 117
    in garages, 109, 110–111
    in kitchens, 106, 107
    picturesque clutter and, 98, 99
    places for, 99
    on stair landing, 108, 109
Japanese influence
    folding screens, 119
    Noguchi paper lamps, 58, 59, 92, 93, 154, 155
    sliding glass doors, 82, 83
    sliding silk panels, 94, 95–96
    on space usage, 119
    wood lattice, 88, 89–93, 154, 155
Kitchens
    bathtub in, 164
    cool, simple, 52, 53
    galley, 158
    lively, colorful, 60, 61
    optimizing space in, 106, 107
    Pullman, 125
Mantels
    broken china, 28, 29
    lowering, 72, 73
    simply adorned, 68, 69
    without fireplace, 38, 39
Mirrors
    expanding space with, 79, 86, 87, 120–121, 152, 153–159
    illusion with, 121, 153, 156, 157, 166, 167
Noguchi paper lamps, 58, 59, 92, 93, 154, 155
Offices, 108, 109, 114, 115, 158, 159
Openness
    sliding exterior walls, 137–139
    wood lattice screens and, 88, 89–93
Oversize furnishings, 11
Patterns
    diagonal, 54, 55–57
    dissolving angles, 104, 105
    illusion with, 11, 54, 55–57
    medley of, 65, 66–67
    vertical stripe, 64, 65

Pictures
    absence of, 138, 139
    amassed, 22, 23, 24–25, 42, 43
    covering bookshelves, 74, 76–77
    creating illusion with, 12, 13
    floating, on walls, 43, 58, 59
    gilt frames for, 42, 43
    papering walls with, 44, 45
    propped up, 14, 16–17, 86, 87
Reality
    embracing, 11, 13, 14–17
    subjectivity of, 11, 13
Reflection
    expansion from, 94, 95, 96, 97
    of gilt frames, 42, 43
Rooms
    color defining, 48–49, 50–51
    expanding, 11, 72, 73, 79
    floating objects in, 43, 58, 59, 78, 79, 141
Scale
    enlarged, 112, 113–116, 167
    reduced, 62, 63, 74, 105
Screens, 59
    double duty rooms and, 119
    folding, 119
    hand-painted fabric, 103
    mahogany, 94, 95
    wood lattice, 88, 89–93
Shelving, 13
    book towers, 113, 120–121, 152, 153
    defining rooms, 48–49
    floating, 78, 79
    stairs as, 132, 133
    walls of, 48–49, 74, 76–77
Sliding doors, 82, 83, 88, 89, 137–139
Space
    cubed, 47–53
    editing for, 11, 39, 114
    empty, importance of, 114
    expanding, 11, 72, 73, 79
    furniture defining, 48–49, 50–51
    illusion of, 11, 13
    relativity of, 11
    removing boundaries in, 78, 79, 80–85
Storage
    bathroom, 103
    under bed, 101
    cubicles, 114, 115
    dressing area, 157
    in-wall, hidden, 113
    kitchen, 106, 107, 158
    media cabinet, 109, 110–111
    optimizing, 114, 115, 116
    oversize armoire, 128, 129
    under sofas, 99
Transparency, 79
Walls
    apartment without, 136, 137–143
    blending fabrics with, 54, 55–57, 166, 167
    floating objects on, 43, 58, 59, 79
    maximum use of, 22, 23
    transcending, 59
    transparent, 79, 80, 81
Windows
    floor-to-ceiling, 92, 93
    inner wall, 13, 60, 61, 93
Wood lattice screens, 88, 89–93

acknowledgments

House Beautiful would like to thank homeowners Kiki Boucher and Aaron Shipper, Elliott and Suzanne West, Greg and Nina Ramsey, Neil Israel, Marc Blondeau, Kathy Moskal, Tom and Pam Kline, and Joel Franklin and Ellen Fondiler.

The room on page 1 was designed by Mallory Marshall; page 2, Peter Wheeler; page 4, Nancy Braithwaite; page 6, Brian Stoner; page 8, Vicente Wolf; pages 10 and 172, Roger Lussier; page 174, James Lumsden; page 176, Peter Patout.

The photographs on page 104 were taken at the Kips Bay Boys & Girls Club Decorator Show House, New York, New York; pages 126-127, ASID Ansonia Condominium Showcase, New York, New York; pages 40-41, Lyman Allyn Art Museum Benefit Showhouse, New London, Connecticut.